SEVEN VALLEYS

TESSA RANSFORD

SEVEN VALLEYS

a poem

in seven parts

THE RAMSAY HEAD PRESS
EDINBURGH

ISBN 1 873921 00 4

First published in 1991 by
The Ramsay Head Press
15 Gloucester Place
Edinburgh EH3 6EE

*The publisher acknowledges subsidy from
The Scottish Arts Council towards the
publication of this volume.*

Printed in Scotland by
W. M. Bett Ltd, Tillicoultry

for

CALLUM

I held it truth, with him who sings
    To one clear harp in divers tones,
    That men may rise on stepping-stones
Of their dead selves to higher things.

TENNYSON

Author's Note

The title of this book is taken from the Sufi spiritual allegory *The Conference of the Birds* by the twelfth-century Persian poet Farid ud-Din Attar, where one of the mystic paths is described, leading into dimensions beyond appearances.

The poem (because the book is one poem) is *not* biography or narrative, though elements of these may appear to be in it. It need not be read sequentially, but is offered as a multilayered experience of the meaning of human life in the twentieth century.

Contents

PART ONE
Search

I SEARCH

On the world's edge was this beginning
so that exploration had to be inward, toward the centre,
a narrowing to the point of utmost precision.

Out on the world's edge, where the Atlantic
protests at a slight land-mass, innocent in its path,
to swell and spume against barrier rocks.

The island here has stripped itself to essentials –
turf, hillock, peat, it has lowered itself in lochs
and humbled itself before the remorseless sea.

Rocks themselves are exposed and striated,
eroded to their bone. In all the earth more ancient
formations may not be found. They gleam with age

in schists and gneiss, in veins of vivid felspar,
quartz, mica, hornblende, and their bed is smooth.
There is no intimidation of reefs like these.

Cormorant and shag, all manner of duck and gull,
divers, waders, deep-sea voyagers above, below
the surface make their home on this island shore.

Salmon, eel, shoal upon shoal of herring,
and white fish, whose flesh is pure as the green deep
waters of the gulf stream they frequent,

bestow a plenteous feast on those who would
live lowly as the ground they till, enriched by shells
and seaweed, brought and strewn in daily tribute.

And the child was born beside the sea,
in a sturdy, stone house on the machair, where
thin soil yields a sufficiency.

The richest crop was people, sheer of skin,
strong-boned, fine-skulled, keen-eyed
and tuned to the turning of the planet

beneath enormous horizons on the edge
where sky and earth tumble against each other in storms
and blackhouses steadfastly shelter,

People whose intelligence of mind
is not divorced from hand, for what they do to live
must be exact or life is hazarded.

Life is in danger and almost stronger
because it is. It cannot take the risk of raising
weaklings. People here live on the edge

and cross over it heedlessly as others
cross a road. To them the edge is the centre
of their ranging livelihood and hardiness.

II LOVE

To become myself I search the patterns
in different threads and colours
some glimpsed only, or invisible
until conditions meet for their epiphany.

That code, implicate pattern
is my predestined order.
I cannot be sure when I've found it
or apprehended a trace,
because as I do it eludes me
again, or rather enmeshes me,
for I see it only in moments outside myself.

[12]

I partially understand and fear
to probe or explore.
It is what I am, a diamond essence.
No cruelty or degradation,
nor even death will destroy it.
It is an enduring portion of the stuff
of the universe, fashioned by layers
of time and space, through fusion,
fraction, friction, partition, connection.

At times it is suddenly, almost hideously clear:
Why did I do it? How could I think it?
Who acted in me? What overcame me?
I was out of my mind or out of my mask?
But the search persists even if it demand
I sacrifice the good.
It sunders me from all I have gathered
and worked for. It strips me
of all I have struggled to acquire,
to clothe myself in, my belongings
and what I belong to —
even the good opinion of those I admire
and the good graces of those I love.

Alone, weak, in pain, ready to surrender life,
betrayed by those I trusted,
I am suddenly given a sign of affection
from a stranger, a word of gnosis.
How do strangers recognise us?
They are able to see us without
our protection in the familiar.
They touch directly the shining essence.
And unexpectedly revealed in others
the shock of our secret,
apparent, reflected:
this grandchild, who must be now
crying in the same anguish as once I wept,
for a cause I do not remember —
whose smile and untaught ability

must be a gift, the gift I gave
as it was given to me.

It is not precisely the eyes, the hands, the hair,
nor can I ascribe it to any outward
bodily aspect of this child.
I know it is present — my secret.
When I hold him I know I am cradling myself,
my own truth, my tryst.
His birth fulfils my destiny
in this place among this people.
I have worked to unravel my pattern,
the colour and quality of each thread
in and out of the fabric of island life,
croft, fields, peats, sea,
the home I have built in this inherited place —

A home, not of stone and wood alone
but of love, purpose, duty, song,
encircled by walls and the bounds
of hill and shore, contained
by codes of practice in community
and church, in clan, in the reel
of families who dance
the measure of human life and rest
in the cemetery by the sea.

It must be this child
who carries my secret
even as I bequeath it to him
now on my breath: may he follow
and find it; may he be guided
instinctively until it is given him
to understand; may he look for the sign
of water and arch. The power of life
must be channelled and pass beneath
the bow of human consciousness,
a dark arc of sorrow,
to reach the coursing river again.

He is born in May, the season of birth.
I shall die and endow him with
my secret, the strength, the entrusted
thing that will draw him, until through him
it is revealed anew entirely
in colours that eye has
not seen —
nor heart imagined.

May he find the self
he must become in order to know,
must transcend in order to see.
May he live long lest he die
before understanding;
despite burning sorrow,
may he live to know the love.

III   KNOWLEDGE

Fear of the Lord was inculcated
as the beginning of wisdom,
a knowledge that, for fear,
never went any further than
this terrifying beginning.

The god was of damnation
whose final solution —
behind stone walls and
impenetrable windows
in the frugal church —
raged from the minister's mouth.

But around the hearth
morning and evening
surely and bravely
blessing and comfort
words for the daily
adventure and labour of living:

'I will kindle my fire this morning
without malice, without jealousy, without envy,
without fear, without terror of anyone under the sun . . .'

Spoken in Gaelic and read in turn
from the testaments by elder brother
or younger sister,
mother and father softly,
the vowels, the blessings were flowing:
'The best hour of the day be thine. . . .'
'The best part of thee that does not grow at dawn,
may it grow at eventide. . . .'
'Be the Great God between thy two shoulders
to protect thee in thy going and in thy coming . . .'

And it is the *deep peace of the running wave*
for the timbers of boats and beams of houses,
nets and creels, ebb and flow
and nine waves for thy graciousness.
It is the *deep peace of the flowing air* —
'as the mist scatters on the crest of the hills,
may each ill haze clear from my soul . . .'
and the *deep peace of the quiet earth*
'on the fragrant plain, on the mountain shieling'
to all who wander and leave for ever,
to all who tend this land, this acre.
And it is the *deep peace of the shining stars*
in atlantic skies above Callanish
over white sands and dark peats
and above each separate home.
'I am going home with thee thou child of my love.'
Who is it stands at the door and knocks
saying 'Open and I will come to thee?'
It is Jesus of loveliness,
'the loveliness of all lovely desires
in thy pure face.'
The deep peace of the Son of Peace.

The future opens as I open the door.
There is a way out. Who is the Way?

'Though I was in weakness . . .
though I was forlorn . . .
though I was without reason . . .
though I was without sense . . .
Thou didst not choose to leave me . . .'

Imprisoned on the island at the world's edge
the boy wanted only to die.
Sea and land, land and sea,
to traverse them beyond his strength
despite his prowess in running and swimming
and saving his brother from drowning.
Yet to die was to burn as the preacher said.
Why should lovers of God be punished,
good folk be tortured, whose joy
and compassion were in poverty and labour?

Were not the fires of war enough
and news of death?
Telegrams bringing dread and messages of heartbreak?
To leave was to die in flames and
to stay was to mourn for ever.

He wanted only to die and flung himself
out of the door into the howl of a gale
and rain and the black night roar of the sea.

He saw and understood.
It was the Son of Peace himself:
'The loveliest likeness that was upon earth.'

He went inside and sat by the smoored peat fire
for the lamps were out
and he never told what he saw
but guarded that certainty
'the loveliness of all lovely desires,'
that bold encounter at the point
where we go so far as to ask for death.

IV DETACHMENT

She would write a letter
to her friend in Valtos —
a letter of explanation for
she was too weak to attempt
the difficult journey
to see Iseabal, home from Glasgow . . .

Too ill to walk a mile
or sit or hold a pen
although a teacher and twenty-one
come home to die in peace,
the deep peace of TB.
She wanted to make certain farewells . . .

Who fared herself so ill
and yet was in control
of the sorrow that was engulfing
her sisters, her parents
as they watched her drifting
in calm visions towards the darkness.

It was this brother who,
sitting beside her, wrote
at her dictation the letter he
did not know was her last
saying: dear Iseabal,
I know you will be thinking of me

As I am of you, my
own, best friend: but I
find I cannot manage to visit
on this occasion of
your homecoming; instead
I send this letter to bear my love.

*   *   *

A boy ran like a deer
bounding from rock to rock,
lithe, swift, over the moor, by the sea:
younger brother, closest,
only two years before
suddenly struck with septicaemia;

jolted to hospital
in Stornoway, welcomed
and joked when his brother visited,
but seemed high, excited,
talked wildly and wanted
to share the euphoria of dying.

It was the last laughter
between them. Afterwards,
alone with that loss of shared childhood,
there could be no mourning
nor carefree running more
but harder work without faltering.

V   UNITY

Stones, white stones, flank the river
washed by importunate floods of winter
        that covered them deep in dim waves
        hidden through sombre days,
and under piercing stars the river at night
        held them closer
in waters gathered densely to roar and rise.

Like seals they lie now by roots of hazel
beneath mossy walls and banks of grass
        or jut up in midstream, scoured
        by forces that drowned
them with melted snow and swollen
        rain slung by gales
to leave them blanched and grained.

These are jewels of the river's making
set to catch the light of spring waking
    with buds of leaves and catkins bravely
    celandines glister purely
duck, dipper, wagtail, chaffinch, heron
    alight upon them sunning
amid the waters singing softly, clearly.

And he understood at once the formula
by which the universe and its phenomena
    emerge to sing again, a dance
    of light and dark, chance
and destiny, each mathematical
    fraction makes another possible
in and out of time, space, turbulence.

Repudiate the enemy, called Hun,
Boche, German: the named is known.
    Our men travel somewhere over the sea
    far away, they die —
and on the island the postlady carries
    a telegram to the home
as death unites what it could not destroy.

A unity for ever broken and repaired
before our minds, remains as desired
    within our hearts, and yet we dare
    to seek another sphere
traverse another boundary in terror.
    What we love we leave, to be inspired,
yet sorrow keeps intact all we hold dear.

VI AMAZEMENT

Who is this girl that has spoken to me and
now I am walking beside her over
the hill along the path? We should go in
single file but we keep together so we

have to hold hands for balance which
makes us one; too aware of each
other to laugh and words are
sounds in a strange voice because they
mean more — more than we
understand of what is happening.

Who is this slight girl, smaller and yet
my elder, who seeks my company and
looks into my eyes as if to draw the
man I will become to his full height;
as if she sees a person I am not
aware of, who answers to my name —
the youth with golden hair? Or does she see
my inherited ache for perfection
and surge of ideals that carries me on the
high tide breaking upon my childhood
and washing me on the shore of maturity?

She kisses me. Amazed, I love her for it.
I hold the secret of my new-formed prowess
as sea-swallows hover dizzily at
breakwater where we stand, or as we
climb the cliffs and far below
oyster-catchers swoop in flocks and
alight stiffly, to pierce roseate shells
with pointed, flaming beaks.

I glimpse this secret self, elusive, strangely real,
throughout the summer months when
she comes seeking me and I imagine
we must share each other's wishes.

Then she gravely tells me of a former love
she has engaged to follow to the East.

I had not known. I do not weep
but nor do I forget.

VII ANNIHILATION.

The boat has sailed. It is into a gale and darkness.
Home and the island are gone.
The future, the mainland, waits somewhere
beyond the storm — this historical present
that is a parturition,
a journey, a crossing over, a passing through.

He stays on deck and the night is universal,
no stars or moon, no promise even of dawn.
He is alone. Other passengers succumb,
allow themselves to be overpowered by the force
of gathered energy that heaves and crests
and devours itself in atlantic winds.
Herring girls and women, bound for the quays,
are lying like a shoal of fish
slithered below, their best outfits
dishevelled, their overcoats huddled
around their seaweed faces.

Captain and crew are silent, geared to sustain
direction and keep the boat at one with the
momentum of the seas. But afterwards,
when the girls are crawling ashore on hands and knees,
the captain confesses that of storms he'd encountered
this was among the worst. Fourteen hours
instead of four or five buffeted on the Minch.
Could there have been some Jonah mingled
among the travellers? Someone breaking
away, yet towards the centre? Someone
searching the wave of history in the present?

The *Sheila*, veteran ferry boat,
midwife to each islander,
she would ride the tides, their fury,
stagger, shudder, quiver, plunge,
but keep her balance in the great high seas.

It is into a gale and darkness,
a journey, a crossing over, a passage through.

PART TWO
Love

I SEARCH

He plunged into the heart of Europe through History,
into its medieval heart, where he found
the clue to the quarrels that still racked

and wrecked the peoples living within its shores:
greed for *Lebensraum*, Spain, Leningrad,
barbarians regimented in Berlin and Rome,

while in Edinburgh's university
Law and Medicine held sway, Theology
with logical metaphysics of the devil.

The Holy Roman Empire was to him
a matter of urgency and papal strategies
to keep the western world wrestling, locked

together in hate and brotherhood, with Britain
and its inbred, internal, private treacheries
a petty offshoot or a last stronghold.

Napoleon affected him: the strong
man from the island, the Corsican outsider whose
vision of unity under law made sense.

And now he saw Britain must defend
the European ideal, for she had built her empire
in the east upon those very principles.

He would serve the greater purposes
of empire, give the world the government it needed
so that humans could live gently upon earth,

without fear of war and exploitation —
yet war inevitably advanced, descended on
his generation as they strove and studied

and dared not make plans beyond the present.
They worked and waited, kept to their integrity
and sought the hidden life-blood in the history.

II LOVE

It was a secret wedding.
He wanted the assurance of outward form
with the daring of secrecy.

His strategy was devised and carried through
without a hitch, except he forgot the ring.
Instead she was encircled in the tincture
of his approval and adoration.

A student of twenty-two and married:
it was unthinkable.
Students were not expected to take
upon themselves such a burden;
and to marry without a home
or income or 'prospects'
was not in order.

To him there was no alternative.
It was as if he had orders
for a destiny laid out before him
clear and unavoidable, yet energising;
a pattern that looped ahead
for him to fill with his self-becoming.

Together they would inform their families
when outward events, when time had caught up
with inward fact, the rush of certainty.

The girl was eighteen, small, dark, intelligent,
vivacious and sympathetic.
More, she loved him and was not afraid
to speak it and trust him.
They met at a friend's party.
She was living at home with mother, brothers, sisters;
he alone, in digs, and far from home.

On Midsummer day they met at the registry office
with her sister and his friend.
She returned home and he to his studies.
Nothing appeared to have changed —
nothing and everything.
They were united for ever and knew it.
Love, though given its rite and legality,
was held within its unspeakable mystery.

III   KNOWLEDGE

The university: entirety
in its diversity
which to know is to be clever
to understand is to be learned
to love is to be wise.

Do we begin with the detail or with the whole?
Do we think with words or speak with thoughts?
Do we learn with logic or with emotion —
emotion, the whiteness from which we abstract
separate colours, the silence from which we utter?

He learnt the names and dates
and charted events on maps
to explore and travel in history,
unravel the stories behind the telling.

He discussed war and famine,
movements of population, the rise

and fall of kings, the
machinations of popes, the whims
of emperors, the struggle
of human beings to find a justice
between the one and the many,
an absolute and its infinite petty necessities.

One afternoon in the library he was drawn
to a book as if it called to him:
It was named a book of verse, but felt a universe.

Deep and deeper it led him
passage by passage
into the rose garden
where soil in its immensity
and tiny granularity,
every valiant stem and delicate tendril,
patterned leaf and stubborn thorn
with insects, birds, butterflies,
worms and clouds,
sun, rain and wind,
in a complicated dance of energies —
flower in the rose.

The *flowering* of the rose is all that matters;
material, it yet cannot be touched.

A bud of knowledge opened in him
and the petals of his mind received the dew.

IV   DETACHMENT

At twenty-three too old:
a notice came by post
rupture to his plan for a career
as diplomat abroad —
the gallant pioneer
Odyssean, wily ambassador.

A shutter came down — out —
he would change the picture.
Why should he sit exams for nothing?
A useless exercise
when Teaching and the Church
played no part in his inward vision

of life at the centre
of action he desired.
Law, too, and Medicine were the reserve
of those with connections
to power or privilege
and he had neither, only his wits.

Silently he packed, left
the student benches where
he'd spent four years taking notes and note
to prove himself an intellectual
with sharp turn of logic
and words at his command.

But what of his purpose?
No-one had ever asked
for motive in serious study.
He left no messages,
wrote no thank-you letters:
exam-time and his desk was empty.

London was the centre
of the British Empire
yet it was tawdry, dingy to eyes
accustomed to colour
of sunlight on the sea
or Edinburgh's pure, northern light.

He would begin anew.
He left his former world:
academic, living second hand.
He simply drove away

reckless, yet open-eyed
into a life that was his to make.

V   UNITY

It concerns the vowels and their numbering,
the sounds they make, the tuning
    of each oracle with its sister sites
    where earth-energy emanates,
and concentrated will-power
evokes a hero for the hour
whose voice rings and resonates —

its frequency captured by Earth
whose daily death and rebirth
    is patterned in stars and their ordering,
    the light-years they are spiralling
through counterfoils of time to join
in the chanting of the OM,
and human music answering.

VI   AMAZEMENT

Letters to write, presents to buy,
people to see, work to do,
food to cook, clothes to wash,
money to find, work to do,
shoes to clean, books to read,
reports to write, plans to make —

and then a baby is born.

Rent to pay, floors to clean,
doors to lock, friends to tell,
a toast to drink, journey to make,
work to do, words to find,

the right words, talk of war,
war in Europe, war would come —

and yet a baby is born.

The woman puts it all aside;
her mind is drawn apart
with the child's insistent suckling
until it is the colour of the baby's satisfaction
on the cheek, its slight movements
and fleeting expressions,
its crying that leaves no ravages,
its hours of perfect sleep —

there, a baby was born.

Talk of war, work to do,
prices rising, refugees,
fuel to find, rationing,
people to meet, letters to write,
money to make, rent to pay,
a health to drink, journey to make —

a baby has been born.

Woman and child make one existence,
new, fragile.
She has been born a mother.

He has been born a father
naturally; it is natural.
He cradles the child in his arms lightly
and takes its weight upon his shoulders.

Separately and together
the three are new-born,
but out of this trinity
again they are forced apart.

War, money, work, people.

He watches the woman with the child
who will feed on his strength
as deeply as now on the breast.

Letters to write, presents to buy,
flowers to give, tea to make,
love to share, love to bear —

a family has been born.

VII   ANNIHILATION

To depart for war is a wrench away
from normality, yet it is to join up,
be joined to one's fellow men, or
identify with those who are banded,
bonded together against an enemy.

To depart for war is to leave behind
the family life and flimsy identity
it has taken years so far lived
to shape and adopt as a self.

To depart for war is to give up plans
and let the decisions of others control us,
and yet it is to decide to do this —
to go forth into the dark, to fly
out into space, to leave the earth,
the habitual, the friendly,
to lose control of the present
in order to gain an imagined future.

He volunteered. He went to war.
He learnt to fly. He took off.
Communication from sky to earth
became his concern and skill.

To go away is to learn how to keep in touch.

PART THREE
Knowledge

I SEARCH

We fly above the surface of the earth
equipped to find what lies below it. We send rays
invisible and swift from a magic box.

The waves are reflected when they meet
some density and a screen displays in pulses
the heart-beat of the prey that we are hunting:

submarines — the sharks that lie in wait
for our ships in the Atlantic, ships that bring
supplies; it is an island we defend.

How is friend distinguished from the foe?
We share a common circuit and momentarily
the tuning coincides and makes response;

whereas the foe is passive, gives only
a constant echo, whose range can be measured
relative to azimuth and height.

The transmitted pulse must have the power
to stimulate an echo in the target, calculate
timings there and back again

with electronic, accurate devices
that keep up with the speed of light, in order to
wreak destruction on the hidden threat.

Detection of an enemy at night
below the sea, behind the clouds, beyond the reach
of normal human senses, faculties,

succeeds through this discriminatory system
made for use against a known aggressor; but we
continue in awareness of friends,

the unseen watch of ancestors, or those
who wait for us, surround us with their regular
responses and signallings of love.

In their sensitivity is safety:
He never thought of danger, knew himself sustained
between the arc of Earth and the zenith.

II   LOVE

Born with ideals —
or born in ideals, for she experienced
the world through a membrane of ideals
which did not break at her birth
              nor as she grew.

To those around her
she appeared polite and natural;
to teachers and mentors she seemed
serene and serious but not
              unquestioning.

Her veil of ideals
did not protect her from wounds
but pain seemed a reminder
of some beautiful world lost, that once
              was Earth we knew.

Sickness, death,
torments wrought by people on each other
were binders for the book of human
heroism, where she could decipher
              perfection's code.

In the name of Liberty
she saw sprawling murder, and all manner
of uncontrolled rapacity, and knew
that Freedom must be freed from
            these shackles of its shame.

            Light was all she saw
as she pursued her way through darkness,
and set aside all encumbrances
of wealth, pride, convention
            to approach the altar

            not as bride
but as priestess. Expertly she drew
the knife and stabbed the monster,
whose mouth spurted the word *mort*
            like a cannon shot.

            In the garden of Liberty
she gave herself as unblemished
offering for sacrifice. It was ordained.
There could be no reprieve
            from the guillotine.

            Her head was severed
but no cut could break the web,
the membrane that, like an aura,
invisibly encased her and held
            her ideals intact.

            Charlotte Corday D'Armont,
une sainte personne, mature
in virtue yet young in years of life,
she returned to the world of beauty
            where she had belonged.

            For she was Beauty,
the disappeared god, who is visible
only against the ugliness we witness
of human degradation − and disappears
            within such loveliness.

III KNOWLEDGE

Creatures communicate sensibly with each other
and control the ocean fathoms: porpoises
and dolphins, whales in their mighty
travels, signal to one another and chart
a course through their limitless element.

The sky, too, is spaceful and spaceless.
It holds no nooks and crannies. To navigate
demands an unearthly sense, another wisdom,
more precise and relational to those
who spin with us, but also constantly
tying us to apron-strings of Earth.

His task was to teach
the laws of communication first of all.
Each man had to learn the rules
and every crew must corporately share
in the understanding. Only by strictly
observing the routines could aeroplanes
take off or return to land. To lose one's place
could lead to oblivion, crashing chaos.

To communicate is to discover an order;
order is creation, a system of signalling
across galaxies or within microscopic tissue.
To revolve around a centre of adherence,
to dance within a pattern is to be alive,
to resonate and sing the leitmotif;
not to know the tune is to disintegrate and die.

He patiently taught the operational signals
and briefed the crews on how to stay in contact.
He was responsible for their knowledge and he
it was who knew where each one ought to be.

A Marshall does not cease to be an airman
with a part to play in the complicated scheme

in which all depend on each other and are
one another's keeper. A leap is built
of tiny movements. To rule is to obey
the necessary connections.
To make these was his task.

IV   DETACHMENT

Pathfinder, you were sent
ahead of the bombers
over enemy territory,
over missiles and guns
to detect the weapons
at long range trained on our heartland.

A student volunteer
you joined Bomber Command,
pioneer, flying week upon week
this time escaping death
next time returning safe:
you won the Distinguished Flying Cross.

Three weeks the estimate
for survival given
to pilots sent out on these missions
but you were still flying
after three months, again
three months and into the zodiac
of fire, the lion's mouth,
August, you found the site
for launching weapons, Bois de Casson.

But they also found you
and the plane was shot down:
another brave young man reported
missing, missing, missing
this time my own brother:
forever we shall remember you,

your happiness, your skill,
your scholarly career
cut short, your sweetheart left in mourning,
your courage and kindness,
your life that flew to death —
missing, for ever you will be missed.

V   UNITY

Within the body of an aeroplane
the crew of six are welded into one.
They become a bird that soars and sees
its prey, that wings and, rising, weighs
along the currents of the wind.
Like cells within a single brain
they interact to navigate the skies.

The captain, pilot and decision-maker,
a second pilot ready at his shoulder,
maintained by the flight engineer,
informed by the radio operator,
defended by men on the guns,
directed by the bomber-navigator —
each one entrusts himself to every other.

To know and do what is alone his task,
to judge when or not to take a risk,
to observe the rules of each procedure
as if they were his own second nature,
to put aside all thought of other things,
to put on a uniform, a mask:
as, separate, they make a single creature.

Helmeted they roar through the air.
They leave behind their weariness and fear.
Their Pegasus a lumbering *Wellington*
together they become Bellerophon
in shining armour riding through the skies,

as soberly against the chimaera
they pit themselves as one being, human.

VI   AMAZEMENT

Three young airmen of Coastal Command,
as every day, walk through the gate
to report for duty, when a bomb is dropped
on the buildings before them; a German plane
unloading before it retreated again.

Three airforce men walking together
three abreast, they talk as they go.
They speculate on the likely orders:
long hours in search of lurking U-boats
in a plane they called 'the flying coffin'.

Three young airmen reporting for duty
shoulder to shoulder and pace for pace
when blast from the bomb kills the one on the right
and knocks to the ground the one on the left.

The one in the middle goes walking on.

VII   ANNIHILATION

It is through snow and wildness –
a journey to make, an ending
that has no end
but stops, choked with blizzard
or waits, short of fuel;
a journey in desolate cold,
absence of hope or regret.

The years of undying struggle
against an outward invader
make us neglect the presences
that dwell in us daily, the life
whose people and purposes
we realise for ourselves.

He decided against promotion and the security
of defence; to live without the trappings
of rank and status won in a limited world.

He packed and caught a train from London to Edinburgh,
Kings Cross to Waverley, through a day,
a night, a day, through a devastated land,
hungry, pinched, blackened
if it were not blanched with ice
and howling months of blizzard.

He knew he would have to make the future
entirely himself from nothing.
Alone, he must find a means
of supporting his precious children
born in the havoc of war,
the brave woman who kept them all these years,
with him away, and waited for him.

He had a dream of his own bookshop
where he would offer to others their secret,
to each one a truth,
the unnamed self, denied and always
surging to find its voice.

The unremitting cold of the famished landscape
rumbled past, as the train
pushed on hour after hour
to the city he held in his heart as home,
although cored even more closely
the island lay, misted and sealed.

It is through snow and wildness —
a journey to make, an ending
that has no end,
but reaches a beginning
which would realise a long-held dream.

PART FOUR
Detachment

I SEARCH

Often weak with uncertainty and regret,
not entirely free from the disciplines of war,
he had gone through the turnstile into peacetime,

which provided no enemy, no ending,
no danger, no orders from above, no regular
pay, no paid leave, no promotion.

Like bullock harnessed in daily drudgery,
blinkered, driven round and round to draw
drops of survival from the well,

his utmost strength was spent every day,
seven days a week, nor could he hesitate
or falter, lest cultivation return to desert.

One day his brother took him, for company,
to visit a fortune-teller, visualiser of lives.

She told him she could see a long journey
through many lands, in and out of darkness,
until he lived by water and an arch.

She described to him the face of one
who watched over him and guided all his ways:
it was the portrait of his grandfather,

exactly as it hung in his childhood
island home. He perceived the face himself
as if he'd always known it close to him,

so close he had not recognised it
or identified the features of his guardian
until now through the eyes of the sybil.

He thanked her and laughed and forgot
her words, until her prediction
was unfolded in the charting of his days.

II   LOVE

I met a poet as I went drinking,
I said to him 'Poet, what will you have?'
He laughed and looked at me seriously,
'A pint of ale and a friend for life.'

Friendship and laughter where he was,
poetry, debate and argument,
wit with learning and kindliness,
songs, stories, merriment.

I met a poet and found a spring
of joy within me I had not known.
The purest water of childhood,
soft with peat and clear brown.

I saw his verses spill over rocks
and seep away into the moor.
They would disappear into the sea,
evaporate into the air.

I cupped my hands to gather them
and set them for the world to drink.
I poured a glass into a book,
And let the city flow with print.

We shared our talents he and I,
of skill and virtuosity.
We spun a line on which to thread
jewels of Scotland's poetry.

III KNOWLEDGE

He wanted to master the craft himself
without help or instruction,
to work it out by fond experiment.

He wanted to pit his wits
against lead and mighty machinery,
the heavy lava-flow of ink,
pressure and revolution,
repetition and precision:
printing.

He bought a second-hand treadle machine,
paper, chases, quoins,
cases of finely-wrought type:
Times Roman, Garamond, Perpetua.

He worked to create
pages of print, handfeeding the sheets
and pedalling in rhythm.
The machine, cumbrous, clanking
iron and steel, yet meticulous
when exactly tuned and positioned;
he, bending eye and hand
to correspond, sustained through hours of night
by brave anticipation
of a page of perfect print.

So − the first poems, the first issue
born in a life-long labour.
He transformed his flesh and blood
into poetry, the handling of it,
material, transferable, shareable, readable −
the book.

IV DETACHMENT

A fact-finding flight by
Dakota round the world
in twenty-eight days, to ask questions,
establish the mode of
signals systems and how
they were organised from place to place.

Names, numbers, quotas, all
deficiencies, all strengths,
an accurate and detailed report −
no time to sleep or eat,
take off and land, take off
again, with dossier completed.

To survey from the air,
to touch down near and far,
night and day, heat and cold, up and down,
people, faces, voices,
travel dizzy, make notes:
the signal system of head and hand.

And the airports call out:
Catania, Sicily
(Mount Etna with its burning crater),
Casablanca's palm trees,
El Adem, Almaza,
Sharjah, Shaibah and Habbaniya,

Karachi's Mauripur,
Willingdon, Bamrauli,
(a detour over the Taj Mahal).
Dum Dum and Calcutta's
human swarms. Mingaladon,
two days at Kallang in Singapore.

A taste of imperial
pre-war grandeur, Raffles

Hotel, the longest bar in the world.
Kuala Lumpur and
Butterworth, Penang,
on to the Buddhist temples of Siam.

Port Lyautey in French
Morocco, Maison Blanche
in Algiers, Tripoli and Luqa,
Bordeaux, back to Britain,
home to base at Hendon,
twenty-four airports, twenty-eight days.

The report was written,
complete and accurate,
after work, in fourteen sleepless nights.
No overload could stress
the working of a mind
alert, precise and without shadow.

V   UNITY

'Robust in his hospitality
of a Friday night, and he works Saturday.'
It was a test of honour
and endurance together
to forfeit sleep,
withold no generosity
to friend and brother.

They would come to his house
when the pubs had chased
them out at closing time
and they were in sublime
flow — of conversation —
appropriately laced
with wit or even rhyme.

For literary
camaraderie,
pleasure in each other's
company:
by virtue of his skill
and strict reliability
he proved them all:

The tall laconic
the short choleric
the gentle makar
the diffident Highlander
the exuberant joker
the voluntary academic
the storied islander —

Poets came for his advice.
He gave it. They found him wise.
He spoke little but they knew
what he said was true.
They laughed, quarrelled — exhilarated
by their own creative lies.
He would return to work and see it through.

VI   AMAZEMENT

One by one they lowered their shields:
those with oblong ones
allowed themselves to peer
intellectually over the top.
Those with leathery targes
waved them aside.
Those protected by bronze
let it clatter down.
Even the almost invisible shields
were punctured in places.

Everyone felt lightened without a shield
and free of encumbrance.

It was as if each were given permission
to renounce the weight of the person
it seemed others thought them,
and could become themselves —
the person they longed to know.

None wanted to leave the company
but when everyday-light returned
they reluctantly marched themselves off
with shields held stiffly in place again.

VII ANNIHILATION

In the midst of life, of daylight,
came death
like the one o'clock gun
with a start, a shock,
without warning, however often it's heard:
a sudden departure
without goodbyes.

But the poet had made an enormous
bowl of punch for Christmas
and friends had clambered up
four flights of stair on the spicy
drag of it
until together all shared a concoction
of words as hot as the drink.

It was his farewell party
although not designed.
He had stood there stirring
the cauldron,
each guest regaled at the stairhead
and handed the liquor of life.

The winter solstice was spent
in flames of defiance

at the separation each one knew
was carried like a ticket
for the journey that ends alone.

In the midst of life, of daylight,
the poet left his friends,
who gradually lost the coherence
he had bestowed upon them.

PART FIVE
Unity

I SEARCH

The story of Snow White and Rose Red:
the children listened, chose colours, painted
the happiness and sadness of the girls.

Really? or imaginatively? The feelings
become colour mixed with water on paper:
from story through heart into art.

But who wrote the archetypal story?
Anonymous: the child in all of us who mourns
the losses that accompany our growing.

Who killed Cock Robin? The child weeps
with all the birds of the air
and death is born, a living pain in her.

On the way to school one day she finds
a dead bird, perfect, fallen from its nest. She stoops,
examines it without the least distress.

This fact of death is not the pain of death
which lurks in her and practises its part whenever
her own mortality is touched by art.

II LOVE

Tragedy, not in love and hate
but unity and division:
love is the longing for unity
we know must be broken
to lead to another more subtle atonement.

Rilke wrote of 'difficult love'
— as if it were ever easy.
The bridge is 'over troubled waters',
waters that separate.

We cannot be joined unless we are at variance,
and the sense of being united is also
of finding ourselves.

How do we learn these things?
We read of the sorrows of Deirdre,
or Abelard and Heloise,
or Mary below the Cross.
We imagine, enlarge
from the severings we have suffered,
and store within us the fables we need.

Our elders feel diminished
in our fulfilment,
as the love they bestow
creates the essential difference
that unites us through layers of pain.

III   KNOWLEDGE

Almost against our will we know,
without being aware, the secret that is our own.

Failures and disasters push us,
seemingly aside, into the thick of it

or we are forced to waste time
in order to live it, and living is then crammed

into a few years, even a few days,
and the waiting lasts as if we were trapped in it

as we are, for lack of looking,
where destiny hurts, and we lazily stifle it.

And the beloved is taken from us,
not wilfully, but swept away

into illness or incoherence or
indifference or private sorrow,

and the practice of silent, habitual suffering
makes us creep, deformed, into the shell

of a self that no longer fits. We hide,
and yet daily expect the end until it confronts us:

death, not our own, but we wish it were,
for the death of others, those we love,
destroys the self we became in that hard-won unity,

and we are left too exhausted
to rally our lost uniqueness and begin again.

We must wait, but openly,
but actively,
but impatiently,

with tears, even shouts, but also
trustfully turning ourselves to the sun of life,

undying life and ways of good, tried or untried,
often unclear, not pure from risk of sin.

We are in the dark and in pain.
Terrors of love remind us
of the secret we shall discover
to lead us beyond the boundary of our death.

IV   DETACHMENT

The poet may lament
gods have abandoned Earth,

for emptiness engulfs the minds of
humans, who feel the loss
and in anger destroy
any trace of beauty that they find.

The shadow of godhead
gathers in monster shape
as if to break the fine filaments
of delicate beauty
woven over aeons,
the habits of love that sustain us.

The youngest child, he knew,
as in the fairy tales,
had been entrusted with his secret,
and he watched her surely
as she grew more eager
in pursuit of graceful perfection.

She rose aslant the Earth,
a ray, almost angel,
with Death eclipsed below her in this
encounter with such light.
She was piercing free the
energies trapped within our dread.

He mourned her folded wings,
her flight that had ended.
Sorrow crushed out remembrance of it,
halted the mind with its
weight, its twisting hopeless
coils of shapeless, angry affliction.

It was a test of love
to believe in the love
she had released by displacing
the divider. He set
himself daily the task
of love — to replenish this beauty.

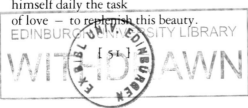

V   UNITY

It is sage: a wise colour,
not vividly green, nor blue.
It is sage: a calm temper,
not loud or quiet, a humour
that holds the balance true
in movement and depth, like a river,
like reeds as they rise and recover
from flood, to sway in the sun,
turn brittle in spare autumn.

It is sage: a fine texture,
not roughly open, nor closed.
It is sage: as if an adventure,
not one that confronts danger
to blazon abroad and boast
about, but hidden, interior,
of intense, unremitting valour:
the secret life must conceal,
that only death will reveal.

It is sage: to heal disorder,
Salvia — to make us whole.
It is sage: to bring out flavour
and complement each other
in arduous renewal,
as the solitary explorer
believes in a land of the future
beyond boundary and age,
eternity now — in the Sage.

VI   AMAZEMENT

Ends tied together to make a loop
loops folded over to make a pattern
pattern repeated to make an intertwined
chain of ends and endings

loops and loopings
patterns and patternings
repeated and reciprocated and

suddenly by a simple twist
or pulled thread released
to a single original connection

the link that made a circuit
a person, a life,
a lived coherence —
love.

VII   ANNIHILATION

To die within a year:
frantic at once:
responsibilities.
Parting hurts . . . with others . . . and most
with the person we know best,
have lived with always: ourselves.

How say goodbye to myself
but go on living? and
give self permission to die,
to go over the top, go on,
walk into it, go through with it,
go along with it, never get over it:
a death that has happened?

It leads, they say,
to golden light after tunnelled dark,
totalisation: all in one,
one in another,
no more divisions.
The moon permeates the deep,
its reflection folded in dark.

PART SIX
Amazement

I SEARCH

Road over the mountain
The only way that leads
Safe through flood and stone

Old road, ancient path
Turns with course of river
Unwinds with singing breath

Gives no shade or shelter
Offers no easy foothold
Cuts no longsome corner

Steep and sharp with thorn
Slippery with scree
That way is the only one

What sign to know the track
When it fails, divides?
The bent tree on the rock

We do not turn aside
Lest we lose our bearing
The purpose in our stride

We keep a steady pace
The rhythm of mercy
Rain on the face

When we reach a cairn
With view of the sea
There the way runs down

Road over the mountain
Highland road we follow
A sense of direction

II   LOVE

It is to lie in your arms
        in the white of the morning
snow on the path, the steps,
        snow on the fence,
chaffinches on the snow and
        barcarole of the wakened river.

Your steady breathing alights on my breast
        as lustrous clouds above the hill
        in blanched blue of the dawn;
and I cradle your slender head.

In long-drawn, slow, slight
        arousal I purely float, held
between the touch of your breath
        and your warm hand at my back.

III   KNOWLEDGE

Snow in the headlights
dances on points
and your hair in silver
swirls in silence we make.

Once you flew through night
of death and burning;
now you drive through dark
to bring me home to your hearth.

To each side banks of snow
and frozen fields, the road

must run between fences
as they define the route.

You are soft with smiles
of love, but strong
as all the terrors
you steadily overcome.

Swiftly I am dancing in
the soft storm of your kindness,
caught in the light of our
travelling homeward together.

III   DETACHMENT

'Take care' we say, although
it is no way to live
and cannot protect body or soul
from the harm active in
every good, but we trust
each other to want to stay alive.

We desire each other
to live and that desire
keeps us living; taking care
of each other renews
our own life better
than self protection.

Some almost betray us
as martyrs dragged to death
by principles or ambitions
that lead them away from
the ground everyone needs
however exalted their flying.

Death is a mocker, has
no respect for our wishes.

Those who ache to die are forced to wait.
Yet perhaps by loving
so much we bring death on —
or by loving we outwit death, dare it.

The road that in winter
brings death is benign
in summer, and battlefields now
are covered with pale orchids
and clumps of tormentil.
Fruit must fall we have laboured
so long to mature.

V   UNITY

Dreams desire to sleep.
In their complexity keep
us awake, and yet dissolve
before we find the salve
that would annul the dreaming,
set desire to leap
beyond itself.

Desire expects answers
to dreaming questions
but dreams, like computers,
accept no hesitations,
seek nothing in return.
Desire seeks her own,
takes headstrong action.

The head has desires
and the heart has dreams;
a wishful thought inspires
fancy's unheard themes.
Sleep makes a circle
increasing in tens
to reach precious zero.

It shatters the breakage
of part from whole,
forms a dark passage
through into the all,
yet is bravely exact
to carry the message,
continue the fact.

Desire shall break free
from the dreams that hold it;
I let it slip —
and waited for it.
I would make my escape:
when the dream awoke me
I was beyond it.

VI   AMAZEMENT

The river must be waded:
each step into the cold current
gropes for foothold
not on flat weedy stones
but in pebbles and gravel.

We stand firm for each other.
We take turns to advance.
I hold as you sway or slip
and you keep me steady.

In time we move more rapidly,
accustomed to the water,
our feet numbed
with treading on rock and stone.

We sense we are nearly there
and fling ourselves on the bank
laughing. We made it.

VII ANNIHILATION

Dawn wings over with seagulls
seagulls scatter light
light is caught in the eye
the eye opens the mind

the mind tags a word
words that say 'it is day'
day and light returning
returning yet quite new

quite new, yet also another
another chance to take
take by making a gift
gift of what I am

I am my own creator
creator of what I do
what I do without fail
not fail to reach the mark

mark my words as seagulls
gulls prise open shells
shells secrete the pearl
pearl of wisdom dawning.

PART SEVEN
Annihilation

The river rampages during a day of rain
and night falls to its roar.
The moon soars among streaming clouds
and treetops dance in the storm.
Speed: movement in counter direction
across the dark.

Enclosed within our ellipse
we hold each other in awe
and protect each other by mutual affirmation:
you, who tease me and smile,
as I watch the edge of fear.

A stone bridge arches the torrent.
We cross it safely, hearing the flood below us.
We climb up steps that end in an archway
leading nowhere. It is a ruin.
When great cathedrals fall an arch will stand —
as triumph over time or a capturing of space.

In space and time we live our span.
From the tunnel of birth we enter
to first unveiling and
through a colonnade of shadows
we complete the circuit and pass
beneath the vault of earth.

Every valley shall be exalted
and the vales removed.
The ripples our life has formed
will be smoothed on a calm surface.

Every mountain ridge that crumples the skin
of earth will be eroded,
the rough places and the crooked
will be carried away until
no trace will be found
of the density life derives from.

We shall have no more presence
than shall reconstitute itself
in those born to our secret,
as we ourselves return to the whirlwind
of who we are, and its still centre
behind the sevenfold veil,
beyond the seven valleys.